Feather Art

Making crafts from all feathers for ages 7 to 107

By Donna Landsman

DeForest Press

Elk River, Minnesota

Published by:
DeForest Press
P.O. Box 154
Elk River, MN 55330 USA
www.DeForestPress.com
Toll-free: 877-441-9733
Richard DeForest Erickson, Publisher
Shane Groth, President

Photography by Brenda Sichmeller

Cover design by Linda Walters, Optima Graphics, Appleton, WI

ISBN 1930374194

Library of Congress Cataloging-in-Publication Data

Landsman, Donna, 1934-
  Feather art : making crafts from all feathers for ages 7 to 107 / by Donna Landsman ; photography by Brenda Sichmeller.
     p. cm.
  ISBN 1-930374-19-4
  1. Handicraft. 2. Feathers. 3. Cookery. I. Title.
  TT145.L38 2005
  745.5--dc22
                         2005021757

*I would like to dedicate this book to my husband, Boyd,
and to the county extension agents and the students in my classes,
who have inspired me to print an instruction book.*

The members of the Friendly Fu Extension Club congratulate Donna Landsman for creating a book to teach others how to fashion beautiful items using pheasant feathers. Her enthusiasm inspired us all. "Limitless talent" is what makes her the fun person she is. Her book will surely be a joy to own, and remember to keep your Dust Buster handy for clean up.

As a member of our club, she taught us to make many things. When the National Extension Convention was in South Dakota, we helped her make pins that had "South Dakota" in the center of a pheasant feather wreath for each person attending. Corsages were made for the dignitaries at a state convention.

Members at that time were Donna Landsman, Karen Lounsbery, Eloise Hybertson, Dolly Swanson, Carol VanderLaan, Vi Nelson, Virginia Peterson, Janet Holmberg, LeAnne Knudson, Linda Holmberg, Mayme Holmberg, Lucille Nase, Tracia Morren and Beverly Andersen. Members today are Mayme, Lucille, Vi, Janet, Linda, Beverly and Corinne Engstrom and Dorothy Overgaard.

The "Feather Lady," as Donna Landsman was nicknamed, has been working with all feathers for over fifty years. Donna has been in many magazine and newspaper articles and has been featured on TV for her feather art. Donna and her husband, Boyd, lived on a farm in South Dakota where they raised four children. They enjoyed pheasant hunting through those years and this started Donna recycling the pheasant feathers into beautiful pieces of art. They are retiring on Lake Benton, Minnesota, where she still makes many items and gives demonstrations on feather art. Donna was in the Ms. Minnesota Senior American Pageant in 2003 and received 2nd runner up because of her talent in Feather Art.

Contents

Contents

Welcome to one of the least expensive hobbies around. Feather art teaches patience and it helps to take your stress away. One of the nice things about feather art is that if you do not like what you have made, you can simply take it apart and start over. You will only be out your time.

A variety of colored feathers can be purchased at a craft store. If you already have access to different feathers, you may use them. There are many varieties of feathers to choose from: turkey, pheasant, peacock, guinea, partridge, ostrich and many more. The most important thing to remember is to not sneeze, cough, or swat flies while working on feathers. You should own a good vacuum and have a wastepaper basket nearby, also.

There is no end to what you can make using feathers—it's only limited by your imagination, and it's a hobby anyone seven years old to one hundred and seven years old can do. So try it—you might like it!

Warning: Extreme care must be exercised when using a glue gun as burns may result. Never leave a child with a glue gun.

MAIN ITEMS YOU WILL NEED

- Feathers—enough of a color you are going to work with before starting a project.
- Flower stamens in a variety of colors
- 20-gauge green or plain wire
- 32-gauge wire spool of plain wire
- Florist tape, green or brown
- Oasis
- Wax paper
- Wet sponge in a dish
- Tacky Glue or glue gun
- Scissors, tweezers

Items Used In This Book Besides The Above Items

Tie tacs, pin backs, wooden or plastic beads, felt, leather or pigskin, leather punch or paper punch, ribbon, bows, 9" or 12" dolls, stiff interfacing, variety of trims, Styrofoam ball, eggs, bells, acrylic paint, brush, stain, crystal clear acrylic spray coating, ceramic pieces, glass or plastic eyes, small table, variety of baskets or vases, wooden bases, crochet thread and hook, box of stationery, small umbrella, hat, glass chimney, pipe cleaner, light fish line, ball-bearing swivel, any pictures showing flowers, pinecones, acorn and walnut shells, cardboard, magnetic tape, small picture frame, vine and Styrofoam wreath, 9-gauge wire, needle nose pliers, plaster of Paris, picture frame mold, dress, clock, and a wastebasket (to discard downy and so on).

- Anyone ages 7 to 107, men or women, can create a piece of Feather Art.
- Be sure you have enough feathers of the color you are working with before beginning a project.
- You may cut or pull the feathers out of a pelt.
- Pelts are easier to work with than loose feathers. If working with a pelt, do not use feathers from a different pelt on the same project, as the color of the feathers on each pelt is different.
- Use tweezers to pick up and place feathers on your project.
- Curl feathers by using the backside of a table knife. Start on the backside of the feather, at the quill, using a light pressure with your thumb as you move slowly to the tip of the feather.
- If a feather splits, just take your fingers where the downy of the feather starts and pull down over the feather to the tip. It will go back to a normal feather.
- If you make a mistake or don't like the way something turns out, just take it apart. You will only be out your time.
- If you loose a feather on an article, find another feather similar to it and glue it in place where your lost feather had been.
- If a feather gets wet, like when wearing the pheasant pin on your hat, just let it dry. Remember, the pheasants and other fowl get their feathers wet through rain or snow, so your feathers will be fine by letting them dry. They will not be ruined.
- If one of your crafts gets dusty, just take a clean or new paintbrush and dust it going down, in the same direction as the feathers.
- If you use fresh feathers from a fowl, it is fine, but keep your article away from cats. The scent stays on the feathers for one year.
- You can store loose feathers in a clean margarine tub but be sure there is no skin on the feathers.
- If in doubt about whether your finished article will attract bugs, you can spray lightly with an insect repellent, like OFF.

YOU WILL NEED

- Feathers of your choice
- Flower stamens
- 20-gauge green or plain wire
- 32-gauge spool wire
- Green or brown florist tape
- Oasis
- Wax paper
- A wet sponge in a dish
- Glue (Tacky or glue gun)
- Scissors, tweezers

1 Lay an 11" piece of wax paper on top of your working table.

2 Pick out three feathers, preferably the smaller feathers. Have one or two extra feathers ready in case one gets ruined. As you get experienced working with feathers, you can use four or more feathers.

3 Cut the feather with a sharp pair of scissors where the downy starts.

4 If you want to curl the feather, do not cut the feather first. Take a table knife, and starting on the backside of the feather at the quill, use a light pressure with your thumb as you move slowly to the tip of the feather.

5 Lay the feathers you have cut on the wax paper to be sure they are alike in color and size. Cut a few extra in case you damage a feather and need to replace it.

6 Cut one 4" piece of 20-gauge wire. When making a centerpiece, you will cut according to the size you desire in the arrangement. Three flowers work best when starting an arrangement. Usually, arrangements have three to five to seven (or more) flowers.

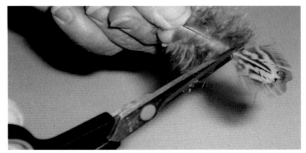

3 Cutting downy

7 Cut a 2½" piece of 32-gauge spool wire.

8 Take three flower stamens and fold them in half.

9 Glue ½" on the tip of the 20-gauge wire.

10 Place the three folded stamens at the tip of the glue on the wire, so the tip of the wire is below the stamens.

11 Hold the wire along with the stamens in your left hand (if you are right handed). Take the 32-gauge wire and wrap it around the bottom of the stamens, with your thumb holding the end of the wire, so you can wrap it tightly until all the wire is wound around the bottom. Do the same with the other piece of wire, only go to the top. This is done so the flower will not come off the wire.

12 Wipe your fingers on the wet sponge in the dish.

13 Place glue on the front side of the feather, ¼" from the bottom, on all three feathers. Use tacky glue for the lighter feathers and a glue gun for the heavier feathers. If using the glue gun, only put glue on one feather at a time as the glue dries fast.

14 Pick up the feather with the tweezers. Place it on the wire near the stamens, leaving the tips of the stamens out to be seen. Put the other two feathers on the same wire. You can adjust them to your liking. If you want four feathers for the first row, add it at this time. You can place this beginning of a flower in a piece of oasis to dry at least a half hour.

15 Prepare four or more feathers for the second row, as you did for the first row.

16 Glue these feathers on behind the first row to try and stager them in between the first row of feathers.

17 Let this row dry at least a half hour also. It is wise to make three flowers at one time so they are drying while you prepare for the next flower.

18 Cut a 10" strip of florist tape. Start at the tip of the flower and wind around the base of the flower and continue down the wire.

19 Pick out three complimentary feathers to be the leaves, but do not cut the downy off.

10 Glue stamens to wire   11 Wrap stamens with wire

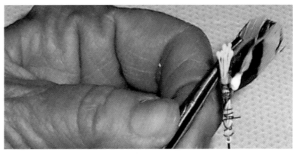

14 Gluing feather on stem

14 Set flowers in oasis   18 Adding florist tape

20 Place one feather (this could be curled before placing it on the wire) on the wire, holding it firm while the right hand brings the florist tape around to hold it in place. Make a couple more twists around the wire and add another feather (curled if desired) with the downy. Proceed with the same technique. If your 10" piece of florist tape runs short, just cut another smaller piece as it can be added on to the wire where you left off. The fluffy feathers are great for leaves for the lighter feathers. You can cut the shape of the leaf you desire when using the heavier feathers, such as turkey feathers.

YOU WILL NEED

- Any feathers of your choice
- Wood base of any size (if using glass chimney or globe)
- Glass chimney or globe to cover the centerpiece
- Oasis
- Any accents to add for holidays
- Scissors & tweezers

1 Make flowers as on pages 10 to 11 in this book. Usually make three different kinds.

2 If you decide to make a big centerpiece, than you will have five or seven flowers.

3 Finish a wood base of your liking. It should have a ridge for the chimney or glass globe to set in so the glass won't slip off.

4 Glue felt on the bottom of the base.

5 Cut a piece of oasis 2" high by 4" square. Press the base of the chimney or glass globe through the oasis. You now have a round oasis to put your flowers in. Take the butt end of a long knife and push gently down through the chimney to push the oasis out of the chimney.

6 Have three different heights of flowers and arrange them in the oasis. Add the plumage, fluff, and three pheasant tail feathers (if using pheasant flowers) or peacock tail feathers (if using peacock feathers). Guinea feathers make pretty centerpieces also.

7 Place the chimney over the flowers and plumage very carefully. If you have to rearrange the flowers, take the butt end of the knife and push the centerpiece out. This is the way you will clean the chimney. The chimney and glass globe help to protect the centerpiece from dust.

8 Glue pheasant feathers to a 10½" long and 1¼" wide strip of brown felt in the same manner as on a hatband (see page 37). Place it around the base of the chimney or glass globe and glue in place.

YOU WILL NEED

- Colored turkey feathers (or other feather of choice)
- One colored sprinkle can (any size)
- Oasis
- Glue gun

1 Make flowers as on pages 10 to 11 in this book.

2 The white and yellow turkey marabou feathers were used in this centerpiece and plumage. Cut the feather to the tip to look like a leaf and use any plumage. Curl the feathers before gluing.

3 Glue on the front side of the yellow turkey marabou, using four feathers. Refer to Step 13 on page 11.

4 Glue on the backside of the white feathers. It will take five feathers for this row.

5 Glue green turkey marabou feathers for the leaves, which have been cut into the shape of a leaf. Or, add the "leaves" when you use the florist tape going down the wire.

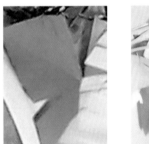

5 Cut green feathers to look like leaves

6 Add green turkey flats, cutting them in the shape of leaves, if you'd like to add more foliage to the centerpiece. Plumage and goose biots may be added to fill in the empty areas.

Daffodil Centerpiece

YOU WILL NEED

- Satinette feathers
- Any colored basket
- Oasis
- Glue gun

1 Make flowers as on pages 10 to 11 in this book.

2 Use white, pink and blue satinettes to make the Tiger Lily flowers, cutting the feathers to shape. The front side of the feather has a shine and the backside is dull.

3 Place the feather on a piece of wax paper. Using a black or brown fine-point marking pen, add small dots on the lower part to the middle part of the feathers.

4 Curl the feathers with a table knife on the backside.

5 Glue five to six feathers near the stamens and curve them downward.

6 Use some light green satinettes for the leaves. Cut and curl them in the shape of a leaf. Use plumage to go down the stem.

7 Arrange flowers in the basket.

8 Add curled colored peacock tail, swords, ostrich plumes and any other colored plumage you like.

9 You can also make these other flowers using feathers: white Easter lily, dogtooth

2 Cut satinettes to look like tiger lily flowers

violet, trillium, wild geraniums, columbine, orange blossom, pasqueflower or Easter flower, bluets, Turk's cap lily, hepaticas, California poppy, chicory, bluebells of Scotland, black-eyed Susans, bunchberry, creamcup, wild rose, mountain laurel, iris, lotus, water lily, fuchsia, cyclamen, tulip, crocus, gladiolus, rose phiox, oriental poppy and many more. The best way is to look at the picture of a flower and start making it by the picture. There is no end to what you can create!

YOU WILL NEED

- Ceramic pheasant or ceramic dog with pheasant in its mouth
- Acrylic paints
- Pheasant feathers
- Glass eyes
- Tacky Glue
- Scissors & tweezers

1 Clean and fire ceramic pheasant or ceramic dog & pheasant in kiln.

2 Paint pheasant either dark brown or black. Paint the beak gold and paint red around the eyes. The dog can be painted the color of your choice.

3 If there is a base the pheasant sits on, paint it green or beige and put a light stain over it. Spray all with an acrylic clear coating.

4 For the desk pen and pheasant (see photo, page 16), finish a 4" x 5" piece of any kind of wood. Buy a pen at a hobby store. It will have a screw to hold the pen in the wood. Cut a piece of dark felt the same size as the wood to cover the bottom of the wood. Glue in place.

Order for putting feathers on (Steps 5-10):

5 Using the pheasant tail, cut it to the size of the pheasant you are working with. Have all the tail feathers ready to glue, as you will glue them onto the pheasant with the glue gun.

6 Put a small amount of glue on the backside of the feather down the middle. Lay the feather on the ceramic piece where you'd like it. Once it is on, you cannot move it. In case you don't like it, than you have to take it off and put a different feather on, as you will ruin the feather taking it off.

7 If you have a pheasant pelt, follow the same order of feathers on your ceramic pheasant as on the pelt, starting at the bottom by the tail feathers. These feathers (long feathers) will go next after the tail feathers are on, but you will put them on with Tacky Glue.

8 Shut the glue gun off. You will not need it until you put the wings on the pheasant.

9 The next feathers are from the back of the bird, like blue, green or gold. Along the legs will be a dark or golden feather. If you do not have wings to use for the wing feathers, find feathers that can be substituted. You will put the wings on with the glue gun.

10 Next, use the brown and white feathers by the wings. Over the stomach of the pheasant will be all the dark brown feathers. Near the top of the neck will be a row of gold feathers, followed by the white feathers. Last are the purple/blue feathers from the top of the pheasant head.

11 After the feathers have completely dried, you can glue the eyes on the pheasant and/or dog.

FOR PHEASANT TAIL YOU WILL NEED

- Pheasant tail or tails
- Plastic mold
- Plaster of Paris
- Green acrylic paint
- Stain and brush
- Crystal clear acrylic spray

1 A perfect pheasant tail may be hard to locate unless you have a hunter to save you one. If you do, the tail should be fanned out and tacked to a board to dry at least six months before putting it in a mold. If you do not have a complete tail available, you can have pheasant tails ready according to size to place in the mold.

2 Mix 3½ cups of plaster of Paris with 1¾ cups of water in a plastic bowl. Keep this thin so it will not harden too quickly, giving you time to arrange the feathers. Pour the mixture into a mold. (The mold I use is an oval one measureing 8½" by 6" by 1" deep.) Place tail feathers three quarters of the way back in the mold so there will be room for a pheasant or dog to sit in front of the tail feathers.

3 Wash the mixing bowl and spoon immediately or the plaster of Paris will harden.

4 Let the plaster of Paris set for one day and remove it from the mold, pressing gently to release it. (Turn it upside down, but be sure to have your hands there so it doesn't fall on the floor.)

5 Wait several days before sanding the top of the mold or painting it green.

6 After painting the mold green, stain it with a light coat. Spray the finished base with crystal clear acrylic spray coating .

7 Cut a piece of dark felt to cover the bottom of the base. Glue this on.

8 Place the ceramic pheasant—or dog and pheasant—in front of the tail feathers. A dog alone looks very nice too.

FOR PHEASANT FRAME YOU WILL NEED

- 6" X 8" picture frame
- Pheasant feathers (assorted)
- Tacky Glue
- Scissors & tweezers

Pheasant frame

1 Cut the feathers where the downy begins. This is an excellent way to use up the odds and ends of feathers you have. No pattern or design is used.

2 If the frame is not brown, paint it brown with acrylic paint.

3 Start at a corner of the frame. Glue feathers around the frame in any manner or design you desire, using tweezers to pick up the feathers and place them on the frame. Be sure to put a small amount of glue on the backside of the feather, overlapping each feather.

Frame for any picture

FOR "ANY-PICTURE" FRAME YOU WILL NEED

- Any picture to your liking. It should have a border of some kind around it.
- Pheasant feathers (assorted or use two different colors)
- Frame to match picture with glass
- Tacky Glue
- Scissors & tweezers

1 Cut the feathers where the downy begins. Be sure to have enough of the same color feather before starting. It will take at least 100 feathers, depending on the size of the picture you have purchased.

2 Glue the dark feathers close to the border going around it, using tweezers to pick the feathers up and placing them on the picture. I use a yardstick, which helps keep a straighter line, and glue the feathers across the picture.

3 Glue the second row the same way using a different color feather. If it needs a third row, use another colored feather, with the last row (closest to the picture) a plain-colored feather.

4 Let your feather border dry completely before placing it in the frame.

YOU WILL NEED

- Cloth pheasant—purchase at a fabric store. They also have different birds.
- Board for the backing
- Frame purchased in the craft store
- Pheasant feathers or bird feathers of your choice
- Glass eye for pheasant or bird
- Pinecones, moss and dried weeds
- Any paper to cover the back of the picture when finished
- Picture hanger
- Tacky Glue
- Scissors, tweezers

1 Press the cloth and stretch it over the board. Secure it with wide tape on the back.

2 Assemble the frame and finish to desired color and spray a clear finish on it.

3 Cut the feathers where the downy begins. It is best to purchase the whole pheasant pelt. Also, purchase the pheasant tails.

4 Starting with the tail feathers, cut to desired length and glue these onto the cloth. Put glue on the backside of the feathers. Continue using feathers on up the pheasant by using a few of each color.

5 Place black feathers at the bottom of the pheasant, using three gold feathers with the black tips going up the side. Longer feathers (usually gray) go over the tail feather, with smaller green feathers after that. Next will be the brown and white feathers, ending up with the gold and black-tipped feathers at the neck. The front of the pheasant is covered with all dark brown feathers with the gold and black tipped feathers at the neck.

6 Add the wing feathers when you are three-quarters the way up on the body.

7 Glue the white feathers around the neck, using tweezers to pick the feather up and placing it on the cloth.

8 Glue the dark purple-blue feather on the head, ending at the top of the beak.

9 Glue a glass eye on the pheasant.

10 Glue the moss, pinecones and weeds at the bottom for accent.

11 Place the frame over the picture and secure with nails or glue. The tail feathers will extend over the frame.

12 Glue plain paper over the back and attach a picture hanger.

YOU WILL NEED

- Feathers of your choice
- Small piece of pigskin, leather or felt
- Leather lace
- Wood or plastic beads
- Leather punch or paper punch
- Tacky Glue
- Scissors, tweezers

1 You can make any size medallion by tracing around a glass, coin or button, depending on size desired.

2 Cut two circles out of the pigskin, leather or felt. Pigskin or leather is the best for this.

3 Cut any color feathers where the downy begins. Be sure to have enough feathers cut to make a complete row around the medallion.

4 Use the larger feather for the first row around.

5 Glue ½" up on the feather on the backside.

6 Using tweezers to pick up the feather, place it ¼" over the edge of the circle. Never put glue on the pigskin, leather or felt, when adding the feather. Use the clock method to add this row: twelve o'clock, three o'clock, six o'clock, nine o'clock (see pattern).

7 Use the smaller feather for the second row. Repeat if needed for a third row.

(Medallions continued on next page)

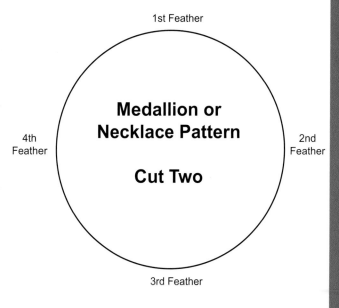

1st Feather

4th Feather

Medallion or Necklace Pattern

Cut Two

2nd Feather

3rd Feather

Medallion or Necklace

8 For the last row or the center, use four or eight feathers alike to make a star in the center.

9 Punch out a small circle on the pigskin, leather or felt with a leather punch or paper punch.

10 Glue the small circle in the center of the medallion. It covers the quills on the last four or eight feathers. Let this dry completely.

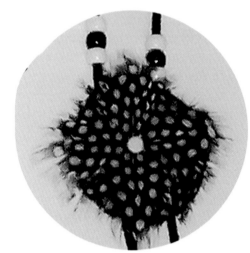

Preparing the Leather Lace For Medallion or Necklace

1 Cut a piece of leather lace 1¼ yards long.

2 String the colored wood or plastic beads on the lace. Put three above the medallion and two or three at the bottom of the lace.

3 Make a knot at the bottom of the lace. It keeps the beads from coming off.

4 On the backside of the medallion, mark a small dot at the top and bottom.

5 Glue on the sides and down the middle on the backside of the medallion.

6 Put the leather lace between the sides and middle, where there is no glue.

7 Take the second circle to cover the backside.

8 Press firmly in the middle and on both sides. Try not to have the glue going over the edges.

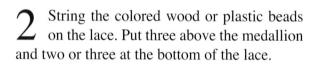

5 Gluing medallion

9 Wait five to ten minutes, then move the lace so it does not stick permanently. You want the lace to move freely in order to get it over the head.

10 You can adjust the medallion up or down according to where you wish to wear it.

YOU WILL NEED

- Feathers of your choice
- Clip on, post or fishhook wire ear-rings
- Leather or pigskin
- Leather lace
- Jump rings
- Wood or plastic beads
- Tacky Glue
- Scissors, tweezers

CLIP-ON OR POST EARRING

1 Cut a circle from the leather or pigskin ¼" larger than the flat base for the clip-on and post earring.

2 Cut feathers where the downy begins or to desired size.

3 Place glue on the backside of the feather, using a tweezers to pick the feather up to place it on the leather or pigskin.

4 Use the clock method (same as for the medallion, page 19) to glue the feathers on the earring.

5 Fill between these feathers if needed.

6 Let dry completely.

7 Glue the flat side of the post and lay it on top of the backside of the leather or pig-skin. Press firmly.

8 Repeat for the other clip-on or post.

DANGLE EARRING

1 Attach a jump ring to the bottom of the fishhook wire earring with a nose pliers.

2 Cut a piece of leather lace (color of your choice) 3½" long.

3 Insert one end of the leather lace through the small jump ring and pull it half way.

4 Take one wood or plastic bead and start both ends of the leather lace through the bead. If it is hard to put both ends in the bead, use a screw-type method of twisting until both ends start through the bead.

5 Push the bead to the top of the small jump ring.

6 Use a drop of glue on the backside of a feather and slide the tip under the bead with the tweezers. If using two feathers, one may be a little longer than the tip feather.

7 If a feather or earring gets lost, it is easy to replace.

YOU WILL NEED

- Pheasant feathers
- Popsicle stick
- Gold, red, white & black acrylic paint
- Crystal clear acrylic spray
- Bar pin
- Tacky Glue

1 Cut the pheasant pin pattern out with a scroll saw on a Popsicle stick.

2 Paint the pheasant beak gold, then paint the entire stick black. Next paint the neck white, then the eye red with a black spot for the eye.

3 Spray it with crystal clear acrylic spray.

4 Cut feathers the same way and place in the same order as on the other pheasant crafts (see page 15). You do not have to use the white or blue/green feathers for the head.

5 After it is dry, turn it over and glue a bar pin on the back. This looks great on a man's hat or on the collar of a ladies blazer.

1 Pattern shown actual size

2 Pheasant pin painted. Shown larger than actual size.

YOU WILL NEED

- Feathers of your choice
- Bar pin or tie tack
- Leather punch or small paper punch
- Leather or pigskin
- Tacky Glue
- Scissors, tweezers

Cut Two

1 Pattern for stick pin & tie tac, actual size

1 Cut two circles (use pattern) from leather, pigskin or felt.

2 Stick the pointed end of the tie tack through center of one of the circles.

3 Cut feathers off where the downy begins or to the size of your choice. Make sure to have enough feathers to go around the pattern to make a complete row. Sometimes, one row is all you will need.

4 Put glue on the backside of the feathers. Use tweezers to pick the feather up to place it on the circle using the clock method, as for the medallion (see page 19).

5 Punch out a small circle with the paper punch on the leather, pigskin or felt.

6 Glue this small circle onto the center of your lapel pin or tie tac to cover up the quills.

7 Let dry completely.

8 Put glue on the backside of the circle (the one just finished with the feathers), placing it on the other circle you cut out. Have the pattern from the feathers facing upward, at the top of the circle.

9 Press firmly.

10 Let this dry completely and add the post.

NOTE: These are fast and fun to make. They are great to give as gifts, convention tokens or to foreign friends.

YOU WILL NEED
(same as for Tie Tac)

- Feathers of your choice
- Bar pin or tie tack
- Leather punch or small paper punch
- Leather or pigskin
- Tacky Glue
- Scissors, tweezers

1 Cut two circles (pattern) from leather, pigskin or felt.

2 Mark the leather, pigskin or felt on one of the circles where the bar pin will go through the holes.

3 Punch the two holes out with the small paper punch or leather punch.

4 Open the bar pin and slide the pointed part through the two holes and hook the latch of the pin.

5 Cut feathers where the downy begins or to the size of your choice, making sure to have enough feathers to go around for a row. Sometimes, one row is all that is needed.

6 Glue on the backside of the feathers, using a tweezers to pick up the feather to place it on the circle.

7 Use the clock method in placing the feathers on the circle, as on the medallion (see page 19).

8 Punch out a small circle on the leather, pigskin or felt using the paper punch.

Lapel Bar Pin Pattern

Cut Two

9 Glue this small circle onto the center of your lapel pin to cover up the quills.

10 Let dry completely.

11 Glue the backside of the circle (one just finished with feathers).

12 Place the circle with the bar pin (wrong side) on top of the backside of the feather circle. This makes the pin for attaching the lapel pin available on the outside.

13 Press firmly.

YOU WILL NEED

- Feathers of your choice
- Leather, pigskin, or felt
- Bar pin
- Black flower stamens
- Tacky Glue
- Scissors, tweezers

1 Trace the larger pattern on leather, pigskin or felt, turning the pattern over so the second piece will be the same when gluing these together. Cut out the two butterfly patterns.

2 Cut the feathers where the downy begins. Any feather you choose is fine.

3 Glue the backside of the feather and place it ¼" over the edge of the leather, pigskin or felt, starting with one feather on the tip of each wing and at the bottom, using a tweezers. I like using pheasant feathers and use the dark feathers for the wing tips.

4 Glue the other feathers all around the outside edge.

5 Glue three white feathers in each corner.

6 Fill the center with colors of your choice. Have feathers meet in center. Dark feathers may be glued going down the center, from top to bottom, of the butterfly. Let dry completely.

7 Take two black flower stamens and fold them in half. Glue the stamens to the backside, at the center top of the butterfly, to represent the proboscis and antennae of the butterfly. Let dry completely.

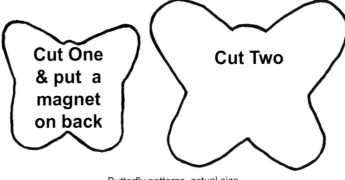

Cut One & put a magnet on back

Cut Two

Butterfly patterns, actual size

8 On the other piece of leather, pigskin or felt, mark where the bar pin will go through the holes.

9 Punch the two holes out with the small paper punch or leather punch. (Same as in the Lapel Bar Pin, see page 24.)

10 Glue the backside of the butterfly (one just finished with feathers).

11 Place backside of the bar pin (wrong side) on top of the backside of the butterfly.

12 Press firmly. This butterfly may be put on the refrigerator with a ¾" piece of magnet (peel paper off; stick to back) instead of the bar pin.

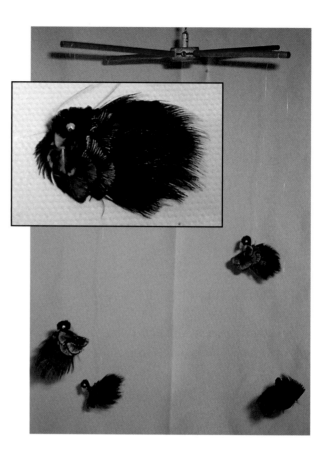

YOU WILL NEED
FOR EACH BIRD ON THE MOBILE

- Pinecone: a long, narrow one about 1½" long
- Pheasant feathers
- Four pieces of 20-gauge wire, each 12" long
- Black pipe cleaner
- Gold felt
- Two moving eyes for each bird on the mobile: 4 mm size
- Light fish line
- Ball bearing swivel with interlock snap
- Nose pillars
- Tacky Glue
- Scissors & tweezers
- Optional: Tinker toy circle and four tinker toy sticks, each stick 6" long

1 Cut the feathers where the downy begins. Use the dark brown feathers. Any light-weight feathers will work fine.

2 Put glue on the backside of the feather. Using the tweezers to pick the feather up, place it in the back (pointed end) of the pine-cone. Use at least four feathers in the first row.

3 Continue adding glued feathers three-fourths up the pinecone.

4 Cut 1½" of a black pipe cleaner. Use a nose pillars and bend one end in a semi-circle to form the head.

5 Glue the bottom of the pipe cleaner and stick it between the small end of the pine-cone.

6 Glue two 4 mm moving eyes to the pipe cleaner head, one on each side.

7 Cut the gold beak from felt and glue it on the end of the head.

8 Glue on the backside of the feathers and lay them flat on the front part of the bird.

9 Tinker Toys make a nice mobile. Just use one wooden circle and insert four 6" sticks. Add a 1" stick at the top of the circle. Drill a small hole in the top circle and glue this small stick into the circle. Tie the 9" fish line down from the four sticks and add the birds.

10 Hang this up on something so it's eas-ier to work when tying the birds on. If you can't hang it on anything, just tie each bird by the neck (as low as possible) and secure it with a knot. Cut off excess line from the knot.

11 You can stick a stronger wire in the bottom of each bird to use in center-pieces or flowerpots. They can be made from any feather of your choice.

YOU WILL NEED

- Half of a walnut shell
- Pheasant feathers
- Cardboard
- Two acorn shells
- Two moving eyes, 7 mm size
- ¾" magnetic tape
- Two plumage feathers
- Tacky Glue
- Scissors, tweezers

Note: Any feathers will work fine for this craft but the pheasant feathers are more the color of an owl.

1 Place the walnut shell on a piece of cardboard and trace around it.

2 Cut the cardboard and glue this to the back of the open shell.

3 Glue the two acorns together to form the head.

4 Glue one eye in each acorn.

5 Glue long pheasant feathers first, which were cut where the downy began. Apply glue on the backside of the feathers and glue to the walnut shell.

6 Glue four colored feathers for the next row on top of the walnut shell, using tweezers to pick the feathers up, and place them on the shell.

7 Glue the last two rows, those at the top of the walnut shell, with the dark feathers.

8 Glue the head to the body at the top of the wide part of the walnut (dark brown feathers).

9 Let this dry completely.

10 Pick out two feathers (plumage) with a lot of fluff and glue these on the backside of the acorn eyes.

11 Cut a ¾" piece of magnet, pull the tape off and stick it on the cardboard. It is ready to go on the refrigerator.

YOU WILL NEED

- Any box of stationery or note cards where you can add feathers to accent leaves or flowers
- Tacky Glue
- Scissors, tweezers

1 Cut any feather where the downy begins and glue it to accent the design on a piece of stationery or note card. You may make up your own flower or flowers.

2 Option: If you don't have ready-made stationery, you can simply draw your own tree branches or flower stems on a piece of paper and add your feathers to complete.

YOU WILL NEED

- Styrofoam bell or ball
- Brown acrylic paint and brush
- Pheasant feathers
- Gold tassel
- ¾" gold eye pin, two for each ornament
- Aluminum gold-colored filigree (gold, flat star)
- Gold string or elastic
- Piece of stiff wire
- Oasis
- Tacky Glue
- Scissors, tweezers

Bell Ornament

1 Paint the bell brown with acrylic paint.

2 Cut the dark brown feathers where the downy begins. (I used pheasant feathers, but you can use another kind if you like.) Have at least fifty feathers ready. If you want to put a different colored feather in a row, be sure to have enough to complete the row.

3 Stick a piece of wire in the top of the bell and attach to a piece of oasis so your hands are free while working.

4 Glue feathers at the bottom of the bell, beginning at the center and working outward to the edge.

5 Be sure to apply glue on the backside of the feathers. Use a tweezers to pick the feathers up to place on the bell.

6 Glue feathers around the edge of the bell.

7 Glue feathers around in rows, beginning at the bottom and moving upward. Be sure to keep the rows even.

8 Glue one alum filigree (gold flat star) at the top and one at the bottom of the bell.

9 Hook the gold tassel through the gold eye pin and stick the pin in the bottom center of the bell with a small amount of glue.

10 Remove wire that was holding the bell. Put a small amount of glue on a gold eye pin and insert it at the top of the bell. Add piece of gold string or elastic through eye pin for hanging ornament.

Ball Ornament

1 Follow Steps 1-3 for making the bell ornament.

2 Glue from the bottom of the ball to the top, gluing the feathers on the backside. Use a tweezers to pick the feathers up to place them on the ball.

3 Follow Steps 8-10 for making the bell ornament.

YOU WILL NEED

- Styrofoam eggs (any size)
- Feathers of your choice
- Brown acrylic paint (if using dark feathers)
- Piece of stiff wire
- Oasis
- Tacky Glue
- Scissors, tweezers

Eggs

1 Paint the eggs brown with acrylic paint if using pheasant, peacock, or any other dark feather. If using lighter colored feathers, leave the egg white. The small turkey marabou feathers work well for colored eggs, plus the pheasant and peacock feathers.

2 Cut the feathers where the downy begins. The size of egg depends on the amount of feathers to prepare, but be sure to have enough before starting.

3 Stick a piece of wire in the bottom of the egg so you can put the egg in a piece of oasis while working, so your hands are free.

4 Glue the first feathers at the narrow end of the egg, starting with about four feathers. This will be the top of the egg.

5 Glue the next set of feathers as though you were laying brick, offsetting the tip of the feather with the one above it so that the tip of the feathers alternate the pattern with the feathers already applied. These do not have to be in rows, but look the best in rows.

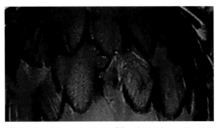

5 Try to alternate tips of feathers in pattern

6 Continue adding feathers until you get to the bottom of the egg.

7 Stick the wire in the top of the egg, and then into a piece of oasis, while you work on the lower portion of the egg.

8 Remove the wire when the feathers have dried.

YOU WILL NEED

- Round clock of your choice
- Styrofoam wreath to fit snuggly around the clock
- Pheasant feathers or pheasant pads
- Pheasant wing feathers
- Pheasant tail feathers
- Glue gun

1 Fit the Styrofoam wreath to fit snuggly over the clock.

2 Remove Styrofoam wreath and glue the pheasant feathers or pads around the wreath.

3 If there are small patches uncovered when using the pads, use loose pheasant feathers to fill in these spots.

4 Cut wing feathers to measure 4½" long. (I needed twenty-seven wing feathers for the clock pictured.)

5 Use glue gun on the front side of the feather, beginning from the quill and out about 2". Quickly put feather on the wreath on the backside. Apply only one wing feather at this time.

6 Cut tail feathers off so you will have 8" tails.

7 Save the tips of the tails to use on other crafts, like the small ceramic pheasants (see page 15).

8 Put glue on the front side of the tail feather, beginning from the quill and out about 2". Quickly put feather on the wreath on the backside. Apply only one tail feather at this time.

9 Continue adding feathers in this manner around the wreath, alternating wing and tail feathers. In other words, you'll glue a tail feather in between each wing feather.

10 When you've completed adding feathers to your wreath, cut the tail feathers to a point. Cut one side starting at the vane with sharp scissors, and then cut the other side the same.

11 Cut all tail feathers to a point around the wreath.

12 Lay the wreath over the clock and push it down over the clock. It should fit nice and snug to stay in place. Since the clock has a hanger, it is ready to hang.

YOU WILL NEED

- Small table, 12" or larger
- Interfacing to glue feathers on
- Feathers of your choice
- Scissors and tweezers
- Tacky Glue
- Glass to cover the top

1 Cut feathers where the downy begins. Any feather will work fine. I used the pheasant feather, but peacock, turkey, guinea, and so on, can be used. Be sure to have enough of the same color and size of feather on hand to complete the project before starting.

2 Cut a piece of stiff interfacing the same size as the tabletop.

3 Have a piece of glass cut the same size as the tabletop to cover the finished feathered top.

4 Measure ¾" from the edge of the interfacing, going around the entire table. Use a white marker if the facing is black, or a pencil if you are using white interfacing. Draw a line from each mark to the next as a guideline for the first row.

5 Continue marking the second row, along with the rest of the rows around, ¾" from the previous edge, until you get to the center. This is done to keep the rows even when going around the table as you glue each feather.

6 Apply glue on the backside of the feather and place it ¼" over the edge of the interfacing. Use a tweezers to pick up the feather and place it on the interfacing. Put ½" of glue from the tip (where you cut it off from the downy) to the center if it is a large feather. If it is a small feather, ¼" of glue is enough.

5 Marking your rows helps to keep them even

7 If the feathers seem to pop up, press down lightly with the fingers so that they will stay intact.

8 Continue with the second row the same as the first, overlapping the feather to cover the tip and glue of each feather in the first row.

9 Finish the center with a star pattern as for the center of the medallion (see page 19), using four or more feathers.

10 Let this dry completely before placing the glass on the top.

YOU WILL NEED

- Any dress or jacket of your choice
- 1 yard, strung badger saddle hackle
- Self-sticking hook-and-loop tape (like Velcro): black, tan or color of your choice
- If doing a jacket, have a piece of material with the pheasant on it

1 Pick a dress or sweater that is a pullover and has no back opening,

2 Place the thicker part of the self-sticking tape (the side with the loops) on the sweater where you want the feathers to cover. You can create any design.

3 Glue any desired trim to the front of the feathers, on the edge to match the color of the top. For example, you might use silver sequins or silver pearls on the sweater.

4 This should dry completely before putting the self-sticking tape on the backside of the feathers.

5 Stretch the feathers or hold firmly while you place the other piece of self-sticking tape to the underside of the feathers. It is good to have another person help hold the feathers while you put this on the top.

6 Place the strung badger saddle hackle on the dress or top. There are many colors to choose from in these strung badger saddle hackles.

7 When doing the pheasant jacket, you would glue the feathers on another piece of material, just like making the pheasant picture (see page 18). Cut a ½" away from the pheasant. Fold the extra material under and press very lightly. Then pin it to the jacket and hand-stitch it onto the jacket. When you want to wash the jacket just cut the thread and take the pheasant off. Then hand-stitch it back on after cleaning the jacket.

YOU WILL NEED

- 9" or 12" doll
- Interfacing (very stiff in black)
- Small umbrella
- Feathers of your choice
- Tacky Glue
- Scissors, tweezers

1 Cut skirt from pattern from very stiff black interfacing. Be sure to put the skirt on the fold where it is marked.

2 Use a white marker and measure ¾" from the bottom of the skirt all the way around the bottom. Draw a line from each mark to the next.

3 Measure ½" from this line and mark all the way around, as this will be the second row. This will help make the rows even. Continue to mark the third row, and so on, starting ½" from the previous row, with the white marker.

4 Feathers of your choice may be used. Make sure you have enough before starting. I like pheasant feathers best.

5 Cut the feathers where the downy begins.

6 Glue on the backside of the feather, starting at one end.

7 Place it ¼" over the bottom edge, using a tweezers to pick the feather up to place it on the skirt. Repeat the same for the following rows.

8 Do not glue feathers on the side of the skirt where it overlaps.

9 Let the skirt dry completely.

10 Cut feathers as before to glue on the umbrella.

11 Glue feathers on the bottom edge of the umbrella, extending the feathers ¼" over the outside edge. Continue gluing on feathers until you reach the top center of the umbrella. If you wish, you may glue feathers on the under side of the umbrella as well.

12 Glue skirt onto the doll at the waist.

13 Glue skirt overlapping one side onto the side with no feathers.

14 Glue smaller feathers of your choice, starting at the waist, to the top of the shoulders. Be sure to overlap the feathers onto the skirt at the waist.

15 Glue the umbrella in the doll's hand.

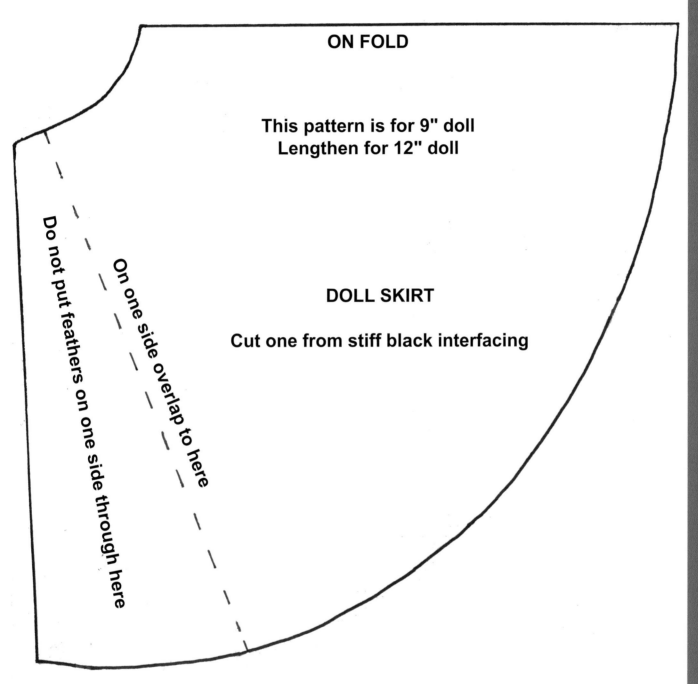

ON FOLD

This pattern is for 9" doll
Lengthen for 12" doll

DOLL SKIRT

Cut one from stiff black interfacing

Do not put feathers on one side through here

On one side overlap to here

Doll

YOU WILL NEED

- Hat of any size
- Ribbon to match
- Bow
- Feathers of your choice to make the flowers for the hat
- Glue gun

1   Glue the ribbon around the brim of the hat.

2   Make a bow to match. You will attach this later.

3   Make flowers in the same manner as for flower making (see pages 10 to 11). As you can see from the picture, I added orchid turkey marabou, small plumage to accent the flowers, and a few hackle to this hat.

3 Add marabou or small plumage to accent flowers

4   Cut the feather in the shape of a violet, or any other flower you like. Then curl the feathers (see Helpful Hints on page 9).

5   Glue the flowers by the ribbon on the hat in any manner you desire.

6   Glue the bow in place.

4 Cut feathers in the shape of your favorite flower

YOU WILL NEED

- Brown or black felt
- Feathers of your choice
- Tacky Glue
- Scissors, tweezers

1 Cut a piece of brown or black felt 1¾" inches wide by 26" long. If you have the hat, measure around the hat and add at least 1" more for the overlap.

2 Cut the feathers where the downy begins. I like the pheasant feathers best.

3 Start with the longest feathers for the first two rows. You can start at either end. One end will overlap so you cannot tell where the band starts and stops.

4 Glue ½" or ¼" on the backside of the feather, depending on the size of the feather you are using. Be sure to use a tweezers to pick up the feather and to place it on the band.

5 You should overlap the feathers on each row so it hides the glue from the row before, but do not put too much glue on each feather. Avoid putting glue on the felt, too. Add feathers of your choice. I like gluing two rows of feathers then switching to different feathers.

6 Glue feathers until you have gone 9" along the felt, then stop.

7 Start at the other end of the band and glue feathers on the band. This end does not need to extend over the edge as it will be covered up. Keep gluing feathers of your choice until you get 1¼" from where you stopped before. If you do not want to put a center design on the hatband, keep gluing feathers down the strip of felt after putting the long feathers on.

3 End feathers will overlap

8 Center of hatband

8 For the center of the hatband, you would do the same as you did for the medallion instructions (see page 19). Glue the long feathers at the top over the edge of the felt strip at least one inch. Add feathers either side by side or by using the clock system. Add more feathers of your choice and fill in the lower part so the feathers look like they grew up from the bottom. Or if you prefer, you can make a circle as in the medallion.

9 Finish the center with a star, as on the medallion, or just have the feathers going straight up. Punch out a small circle from another piece of felt or leather using the paper punch. Glue this in the center of your design for the finishing touch on your hatband.

10 Let dry completely before putting it on the hat.

11 The medallion center will go in the front of the hat. Wrap it around the hat and pull snuggly. Glue on the under side of the long feather end and press over the top of the other end. The long feathers will cover up this seam.

YOU WILL NEED

- A plain mask of your choice that you have made (see pattern) or purchased
- Feathers of your choice
- Any trim of your choice
- 13" elastic string for eye mask
- 14" strung chinchilla saddle for the face mask
- Paper punch
- Tacky Glue

1 For the eye mask, cut pattern (facing page) from a piece of firm poster board. Or, you can purchase a face mask.

2 Cut feathers where the downy begins. Be sure to have enough feathers of your choice before starting.

3 Glue feathers on the backside. If making the eye mask, start at the top of the mask and place feathers ½" from the edge so that the tip of the feather extends beyond the pattern. Continue gluing feathers around the outside of the mask.

4 If using large feathers, it will only take two rows around for the face mask. If smaller feathers are used, you'll need three rows.

5 Glue small feathers around the eyes.

6 Punch a hole with a paper punch on each side of the eye mask. Tie a 13" piece of elastic through each hole.

7 If you prefer, you can glue a stick on the side of the mask (see photo) instead of using elastic.

8 If making the face mask, glue 14" of strung chinchilla saddle around the outside of the mask.

9 It is fun to create any design. You can also add other pieces you've made to your face mask, such as a butterfly (see page 25).

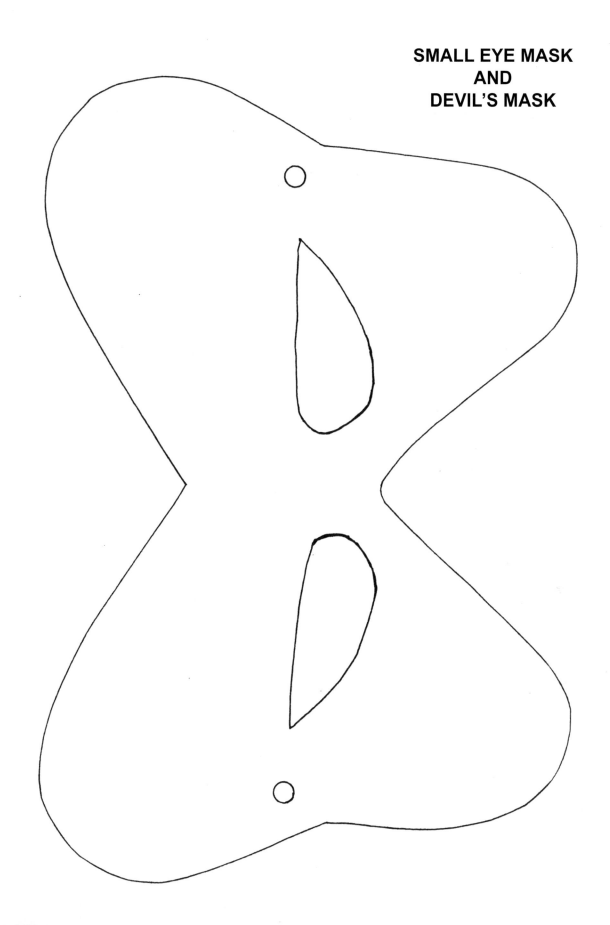

**SMALL EYE MASK
AND
DEVIL'S MASK**

Masks

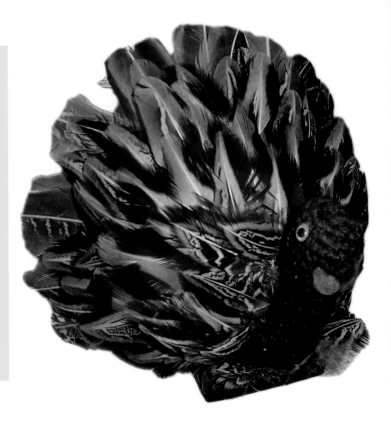

YOU WILL NEED

- Pheasant wing feathers, or any other brown feathers that resemble a turkey
- 3" Styrofoam ball
- Two pieces of 9-gauge wire, each 2" long
- 2" square piece of wood
- Brown acrylic paint and brush
- No. 6 steel crochet hook
- Brown crochet thread
- Red felt
- Two glass eyes
- Awl or large nail
- Tacky Glue or glue gun
- Scissors, tweezers

1 Cut two pieces of 9-gauge wire 2" long each to use for the legs.

2 Stick wire into the Styrofoam ball ½" using a small amount of glue on each side.

3 Glue the other end of the wire into the square piece of wood. You may first have to use a hammer and nail to make two holes in the wood for the wire legs.

4 Paint the Styrofoam ball brown with acrylic paint.

5 Use the wing feathers from the pheasant, or if you do not have these, you can use the tail feathers or any brown feathers that resemble the color of a turkey.

6 Draw a circle with a black marker on the Styrofoam ball toward the back. A ring from a canning jar works well. This will be the first row for the back of the turkey.

7 Draw a second line ½" from the first line and continue to mark for each row until you are at the front.

8 Pre-punch a hole in the Styrofoam on the marked circle with an awl or large nail before inserting wing feathers so the feathers don't break.

9 Put at least ½" of glue on the quill end of the feather and stick it in the hole you just made. Continue around the line marked, spacing each feather ½" apart. Do not worry about the feathers being different lengths as you will cut these down to 2½" after you have the turkey completed.

10 Glue feathers for two to three more rows in the same manner of following the circles.

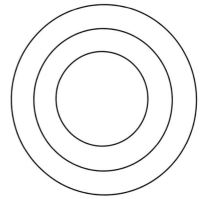

6 Draw rings ½" apart on Styrofoam ball as guide for placing feathers.

11 Glue the feathers on the side so they will drag on the table or close to the piece of wood.

12 Glue plumage or pheasant fluff at the tail end of the turkey.

13 Glue smaller feathers toward the front of the turkey, in front of those already placed.

14 At the very front of the turkey, first glue the feathers on the backside. Place them flat to the Styrofoam ball.

15 Cut the back feathers so they are 2½" high. If the other feathers in front of the back feathers seem too high, just cut the row shorter than the last row. Be sure you have used feathers of the same color.

Wattle pattern, actual size

MAKING THE TURKEY HEAD

16 With a #6 steel crochet hook, work as tightly as possible using dark brown thread.

- Ch 2 (chain next to hook is turning chain)
- Round 1: 6 sc in 2nd ch from hook. Do not join rounds.
- Round 2: Skip turning chain, 2 sc in each st (12 sts.)
- Round 3: Increase every other st (18 sts.)
- Beak: Ch 4, slip st in 4th chain from hook.
- Round 4: Work 1 round even (18 st.)
- Round 5: Skipping turkey beak, work even to back of head—that is, directly opposite beak. Decrease 1 st, work even to front (17sts.)
- Round 6: Work 1 round even, (17 sts.)
- Round 7: Decrease 1 st at front of head (16 sts.)
- Round 8 & 9: Work even (16 sts.)
- Round 10: Decrease 1 st at back of head (15 sts.) Work even for 8 more rounds.
- Round 19: 4 sc, chain 1, turn. 2 sc in first st, 1 sc, 2 sc in next st, 1 sc in next, 2 sc in next, chain 1, turn. Sc in next 2 st, 2 sc in next, sc to end; chain 1, turn.
- Next row; sc in each st across; turn.
- Next row; sc across, fasten off and weave in end.

17 Fill the head with cotton.

18 Glue the glass eyes, but clip the tips off with a toenail clipper.

19 Cut two pieces of red felt for the wattles (see pattern above). Glue these to the lower part of the head so they hang below the head.

20 Glue the head and neck of the turkey to the body. The glue gun works nicely for this.

21 Add more feathers where the neck meets the body to cover the area you just glued.

YOU WILL NEED

- Any size purse you like
- Feathers of your choice
- Stamens
- Tacky Glue
- Scissors, tweezers

1 Cut your feathers to the size desired for the purse you are decorating.

2 Cut off the tips of the stamens ¼" from the stamens. Glue stamens for the center of the flower.

3 Start a row of feathers around the stamens, gluing on the backside of the feather.

4 If you want several rows of feathers on your purse, start away from the stamens (like a ½") and glue up to the stamens.

5 This is a very simple way to decorate a purse. If you lose a feather while using the purse, it is very easy to replace. Just lift a feather up and glue another feather in its place.

3 Various flower patterns

FOR PHEASANT WREATH YOU WILL NEED

- Styrofoam ring of your choice
- Pheasant pads (buy at the craft store)
- Loose feathers, if desired
- Bow of your choice

Pheasant wreath

1 If you want a pheasant wreath or a wreath made from feathers from another bird, purchase a Styrofoam ring in the size of your choice.

2 Glue the pheasant pads on the ring, over-lapping each one as you go around. If you use loose feathers, glue each feather on the ring, one by one, overlapping them as you go around the ring. This is done similar to the Sty-rofoam ring on the clock (see page 31) if you use the pads.

3 You may add pheasant tails, curling them in any direction, or a butterfly or a flower. It's fun to create a unique wreath that no one else has.

FOR NEVER FAIL BOA WREATH YOU WILL NEED

- 58" of 9-gauge wire
- Natural hackle boa strung (it comes 60" long)
- Bow

Never Fail Boa wreath

1 Make a circle with the 9-gauge wire and solder the ends together. Make a small loop on the top of the circle for a hook, leaving ¼" opening in the loop.

2 There will be a small loop at each end of the natural hackle boa. Hook one end over the loop on the top of the wire.

3 Go in and out of the circle, winding the boa around the wire.

4 Hook the loop on the tail end of the boa hackle over the hook where you started.

5 Wire a large bow where the hook is.

There are many colored boas to choose from, so it is fun to make. It is easy to take apart, also.

While this may seem like a strange section to add to a book on feather art, I realized after talking to many people that some never learned the correct way to dress (or undress, it would seem) a pheasant. Whether you're a hunter following the rule, "You shoot it, you clean it," or if you're simply the designated cook that needs to clean a pheasant, the step-by-step instructions below will help you prepare your pheasant like an expert, whether you're eating the bird (see pages 46-47 for special recipes) or using the beautiful pelt for feather art. The same method works for any fowl as well.

1 Cut the wings and feet off the fowl. Cut legs off where the feathers start (see photo 1a). Then cut the wings off at the joint (see photo 1b). Tin sheers work well. Next, cut the tail off by holding the long feathers back with one hand and taking a sharp knife and cutting the tail section off in one piece (see photo 1c). If the tail is in perfect order and no tail feathers are missing, you can stretch the tail open and attach it with a thumbtack on a board to dry. You can add borax on the fat part of the tail. Be sure to put it where cats cannot reach it!

2 Cut into the skin above the white feathers on the neck for a pheasant (see photo 2).

3 Cut, or put your thumbs inside and tear down (see photo 3), over the stomach area. This area is just black, fluffy feathers. Pull the skin down with your fingers over the wing area and keep pulling it down until it is off the bird. This skin should come off in one piece unless it is an old fowl. The older birds will have a long tail and the skin will pull off much harder. If you tear the skin, you can still use it.

4 If it is a pheasant, leave the head (or a leg) on the bird for transporting it. Otherwise, cut the head off and finish removing the inside (see photos 4a and 4b), washing it thoroughly. Be sure you have pulled the top purple and blue feathers off the head as you can use these also.

Photo 1a

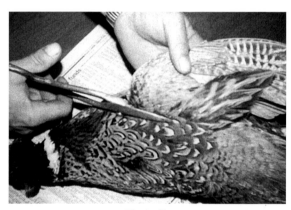
Photo 1b

Photo 1c

5 Lay the pelt on a board, feather side down. Stretch the pelt and use thumbtacks or a staple gun through the skin to attach the pelt to the board (see photo 5). Use one tack or staple in each corner and two at the neck edge.

6 Generously sprinkle Borax all over the skin (see photo 5). Try not to get too much on the feathers. If you plan to use the feathers right away, you do not need to use Borax.

7 After the pelts have dried a week, take them off the board. To store them, take two pelts and put the skin sides together and lay them in a box. Take the next two pelts and do the same, laying them on the first two. Continue adding pelts in this manner until the box is full. Add mothballs all over the pelts and store where animals cannot get to them. (Spiders love pelts; mothballs will keep them away.) Every year, if you still have not used the pelts, add another box of mothballs. Storing pelts in this way will help them last for years. Never put pelts in plastic bags.

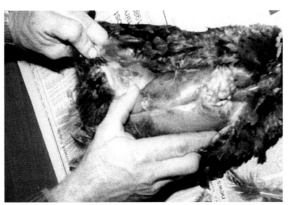
Photo 4a

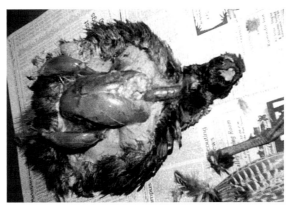
Photo 4b

Photo 2

Photo 5

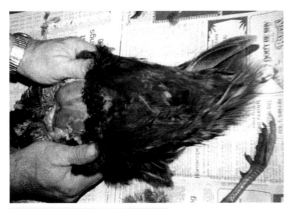
Photo 3

Never Fail Pheasant

- 1 pheasant, cut in serving pieces
- 1 cup flour
- 1 tsp. of salt
- ¼ tsp. pepper
- ½ cup margarine
- 2 cans mushroom soup (or golden mushroom soup)
- 1½ cups of warm water

Cut the pheasant like you cut chicken. Put 1 cup flour in a plastic bag. Add 1 tsp. of salt and ¼ teaspoon of pepper to the flour. Shake the bag so it is mixed well.

Have a large frying pan or electric skillet on medium heat with ½ cup of margarine melted in it. Place two pieces at a time in the bag of flour and shake. Take them out and place them in the hot margarine. Take two more pieces and do the same until all the pieces are in the pan to brown. Turn each piece over until all is brown.

In a bowl combine two cans of mushroom soup to 1½ cups of warm water. Mix well. Add this mixture to the pheasant in the pan. Turn the heat on low for one hour if it is a young bird or two hours if it is an older bird. You may have to add more water if it gets too low in the pan. The soup mixture is then used for gravy when ready to serve.

Creamed Pheasant

- 1 pheasant, cut in serving pieces.
- ½ cup shortening
- 2 cups onions
- 1 cup light cream
- ½ cup flour

Clean pheasant and cut in serving pieces Wild game may be soaked in very cold salt water for 2 hours or overnight. Place the pheasant in flour seasoned with salt and pepper. Brown meat slowly on both sides in hot shortening. Top with onions; pour over 1 cup water. Cover tightly and cook on top of stove over low heat or bake in slow oven (325 degrees) until tender, about one hour if it is a young pheasant, longer if it is an older pheasant. Twenty minutes before the pheasant is done, pour light cream over it. Serve creamed pheasant over potatoes.

Pheasant Casserole

- 1 cup dry brown rice
- 1 pkg. dry Lipton onion soup
- 2 cans cream of chicken soup
- 2 cans or more of water
- Crushed cracker crumbs.

Boil pheasant until done and cut into bite size pieces.

Put rice in bottom of a greased 9" x 13" glass pan. Top with pieces of pheasant.

Mix onion soup, cream of chicken soup, and water together. Pour over the pheasant and rice. Top with crushed cracker crumbs. Cover with foil and bake two hours or more at 300 degrees.

Pheasant Bar-B-Que

- 1 can tomato soup
- 1½ cups ketchup
- 3 tbsp. brown sugar
- 3 tbsp. vinegar
- 2 tsp. chili powder
- 3 tsp. Worcestershire sauce
- 1 medium onion
- ½ cup water
- 1 pheasant, cut in serving pieces

Combine all the ingredients listed above in the order given, except for the pheasant, to make the sauce.

Cut pheasant in serving pieces, brown well, then pour sauce over it and simmer or bake at 300 degrees for 2½ hours. Add water if needed.

Roasted Pheasant

- 1 pheasant, cut into serving pieces
- 1 tsp. salt
- ¼ tsp. pepper
- ½ cup cooking oil
- ¾ cup flour
- 1 cup sweet cream
- Small amount of white cooking wine (if desired)

Coat all sides of the pheasant pieces with the flour and salt and pepper, which have been mixed together. Brown in the hot oil. Arrange the pieces in a casserole and add the sweet cream. Cover and bake in an oven at 375 degrees for two hours or until tender. Add water as needed. Baste occasionally with the cream and drippings mixture. Add the small amount of wine about 30 minutes before the end of the baking time. The wine tenderizes and adds flavor.

Pheasant Dressing Bake

I like to use this recipe cooking the older pheasants. Cut the pheasant in pieces and boil it until done. Cool the meat until you can handle it and cut it in bite size pieces.

- 1 cup milk
- 2 cans cream of chicken soup
- 1 can cream of mushroom soup

Mix the following together:
- 2 pkg. (7 or 8 oz.) herb seasoned stuffing mix
- 1 can cream of mushroom soup
- 4 cups broth (juice pheasant was cooked in)
- 4 well-beaten eggs
- Mushrooms, if desired

Mix and spread this in a 9" x 13" greased cake pan. Top with 5 cups of diced cooked pheasant.

Combine 1 cup milk, 2 cans of cream of chicken soup, 1 can of cream of mushroom soup and pour over all.

Cover with foil. Bake at 350 degrees for 45 minutes or until set.

Please copy this page, add the necessary information, and mail it with your check or money order, payable to Donna Landsman, to:

Donna Landsman
2035 North Shore Dr.
Lake Benton MN 56149

ISBN: 1-930374-19-4
Feather Art $19.95 each   Qty. _____

Total: _____

MN residents add 6.5% sales tax ($1.30/book) _____

Shipping: $3.00 first book, $1.50 each additional _____

Total enclosed: _____

Name: _____

Address: _____

City: _____ State: _____ Zip: _____

Phone: (__) _____ Email:_____

You can also order this book from DeForest Press at
www.DeForestPress.com, or by calling toll-free 1-877-441-9733.